DISCARDED
Science Experiments
WITH
SOUND

Sally Nankivell-Aston
and Dorothy Jackson

W
FRANKLIN WATTS
A Division of Grolier Publishing
NEW YORK • LONDON • HONG KONG • SYDNEY
DANBURY, CONNECTICUT

Picture credits
Tony Stone Images 4 (tr Tom Tietz; mc Tim Davis), 25
(tl Chuck Davis), 29 (bl MacNeal Hospital); Tony
Stone Worldwide 14 (bl Mike Vines); Rex Features 4
(mr Nils Jorgensen), 11 (bl Nils Jorgensen), 18 (bl
Alix/Panie), 23 (mr); Image Bank 5 (bl Don Klumpp),
17 (mr Steve Niedorf), 27 (bl Jaime Villaseca); The
Stock Market 8 (bl Ned Gillette), 12 (bl Jean Miele);
Science Photo Library 21 (mr Charles D. Winters).

Thanks, too, to our models: Nicola Blackman, Mica
Dhyll, Aaron Gupta, George Marney, Thomas Sipi,
Ahmani Vidal-Simon, Beau-Bart Von Haidenthaler,
David Watts and Amy Willoughby.

Editor: Claire Berridge
Art director: Jonathan Hair
Designer: Mo Choy
Photography: Ray Moller (unless otherwise credited)
Artwork: Peter Bull
Cover photography: Steve Shott

First published in 1999 by Franklin Watts

First American edition 2000 by Franklin Watts
A Division of Grolier Publishing
90 Sherman Turnpike
Danbury
CT 06816

Visit Franklin Watts on the Internet at:
http://publishing.grolier.com

Nankivell-Aston, Sally.
    Science experiments with sound / Sally Nankivell-Aston and
Dorothy Jackson. -- 1st American ed.
        p. cm.
    Includes index.
    Summary: Explores the properties of sound, through experiments
using materials that are readily available in both homes and
schools.
    ISBN 0-531-14578-6 (hbk.) -- ISBN 0-531-15431-9 (pbk.)
    1. Sound--Experiments Juvenile literature. [1. Sound-
-Experiments. 2. Experiments.] I. Jackson, Dorothy (Dorothy M.)
II. Title.
QC225.5.N36 2000
534'.078--dc21
                                99-38246
                                CIP

Contents

Sounds All Around

IT IS VERY DIFFICULT TO IMAGINE a world without sound. Our world is full of lots of different sounds — some you will like, some you won't, some that are natural, some that are made by people or machines. Some sounds are made for a reason – to communicate, to give pleasure, or to warn of danger. Other sounds just happen. All sounds are caused by something vibrating. We hear the sounds because the vibrations travel through the air to our ears.

What is the source of sound in each picture? Can you describe the different sounds you would hear from each sound source?

4

Be Amazed

By doing the experiments in this book, you can learn some amazing things about sound. You will find out how sounds behave, how we hear them, and lots of other interesting facts. Some experiments may answer questions that you already ask about sound. Some may make you think of more!

Look Closely

Scientists always ask lots of questions and observe carefully. That includes looking, feeling, and listening. When you are doing the experiments, look closely to see what is happening. Don't be upset if your predictions do not always turn out to be correct, as scientists (and that includes you!) learn a lot from unexpected results.

Be Careful

Always make sure an adult knows that you are doing an experiment. Ask for help if you need to cut, saw, or use heavy, sharp, or electrical items. Very loud sounds can damage your hearing, so be careful. Follow the step-by-step instructions carefully, and remember — be a safe scientist!

Sound Detectives

WHEN YOU ARE GIVEN PRESENTS on your birthday, have you ever tried to guess what is inside before you unwrap them? If the present is in a box, then it is difficult to get clues by looking at the shape. So, you might listen to the sounds made by the object inside as you move the present around. Find out how good a friend is at guessing what is inside some mystery boxes.

1 Make four mystery boxes by putting one object inside each box, and then wrap the boxes with the paper.

In Action

Special sound effects are made for plays in schools and theaters and on the radio. Often the object used to make the sound effect is nothing like the real sound source!

2 Give the boxes to your friend, and ask him or her to listen to the sounds made by the object inside as he or she tips each box gently from side to side. Do the sounds tell them about the way the objects move? Which objects roll? Which objects slide? Can any slide and roll?

3 Ask your friend to turn the box over and over. What sound does each object make when it drops inside the box? Which objects sound heavy and which sound light?

4 Now ask your friend to shake the boxes. What sound does each object make when shaken? Using these sound clues, can they guess what object is inside each box?

Keep Thinking

When you cross a road, you are told to stop, look, and listen. What sorts of sounds would tell you it was unsafe to cross? What noise do you hear when large vehicles are reversing? Why do you think they make this noise?

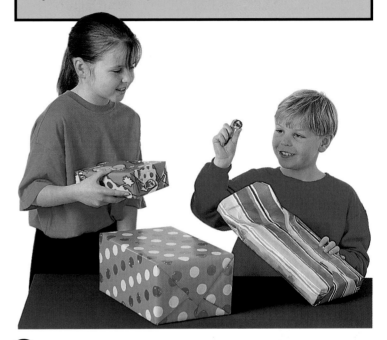

5 Open the mystery boxes and find out! Is your friend good at being a sound detective?

Don't Stop There

● Use a tape recorder to make a cassette tape of different everyday sounds that you can hear around your home or school. Play the tape to some friends, and find out how many of the sounds they can identify.

● Sit in a yard or school playground. Close your eyes for 10 minutes and listen carefully. Make a list of all the sounds you hear. Which sounds do you like? Which do you dislike?

Seeing Sound

SOUND IS NOT SOMETHING that you can see — you only hear it. However, by doing the following experiment, you can "see" the effect of sound vibrations. Make sure you get permission from an adult to do this experiment.

✓ You will need
- ✓ a stereo system with loudspeakers
- ✓ a metal biscuit or cake pan (without lid)
- ✓ a tape or CD of dance music
- ✓ rice

1 Put one of the loudspeakers on its back. Place the can upside down on top of the speaker, over the place the sound comes out.

2 Now put some rice on top of the upside-down can.

In Action

Sometimes sound vibrations can be very useful. In many ski resorts, the vibrations from the sound of an explosion are used to start avalanches deliberately during the night so that slopes are safe for skiers the next morning.

3 Play some dance music on your stereo system. Choose a track that has a heavy beat (bass line) in it. Play the music quietly at first, then slowly turn up the volume until the rice dances to the music!

4 What happens if you turn the volume up a bit more? What do the rice grains do now? Be careful — if the music is too loud, it could damage your hearing. Why do you think the rice dances in this way?

 Don't Stop There

● Find out what other things "dance" to the music. Repeat the experiment using foods such as sugar, salt, cornmeal, flour, or cookie decorations. Which type of food "dances" best?

● You can also see the effect of sound vibrations using a tuning fork. Hold the fork at one end and bang the forked end on a table edge. Quickly put the forked end into a bowl of water. What do you notice?

Feeling Sound

YOU CAN FEEL SOUND vibrations as well as seeing the effect of them. Some people who are deaf dance in time to music by feeling the vibrations sounds make. Find out more about the feel of sound in this experiment.

✓ **You will need**
✓ a large round balloon

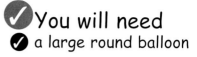

1 Blow up the balloon and tie it. Hold it by the knot.

2 Ask a friend to put his or her hand against one side of the balloon.

3 Put your mouth against the other side of the balloon. Say the letters of the alphabet slowly and clearly.

4 Find out which of the sounds your friend can feel most easily. You might like to record your results in a table. What is the sound traveling through inside the balloon?

Don't Stop There

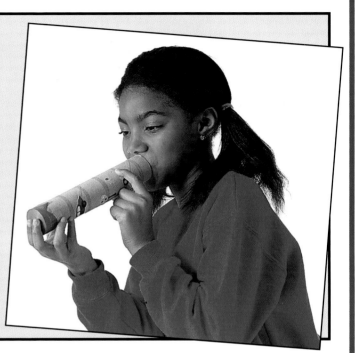

● Now fill a balloon with water and do the experiment again. Can you still feel the vibrations from the sounds? Can sound travel through water?

● Cut open a large balloon (that has not been blown up) and stretch it over one end of a long cardboard tube. Hold it in place with tape. Put your hand on the balloon and talk into the other end of the tube. Can you feel the vibrations?

In Action

Evelyn Glennie is a world-famous percussionist. She is also deaf but manages to "hear" music by feeling the vibrations made by the instruments.

Keep Thinking

There is a special alarm clock for people who are deaf. Instead of ringing, the clock vibrates. Where do you think people who use this type of clock put it during the night so the vibrations wake them up in the morning?

Sound on the Move

SOUND VIBRATIONS TRAVEL through the air in waves. The experiment below will give you a good idea of how these waves of sound travel. The Slinky represents a sound wave.

✓ **You will need**
✓ a Slinky (coiled-spring) toy

1 Ask a friend to hold one end of the Slinky and stretch it across the top of a table. Hold the other end yourself.

2 Quickly pull your end of the Slinky backward and forward, in a sharp movement. In this way, you are acting like a vibrating sound source. Look closely to see what happens. Can you see a wave traveling from your end of the Slinky to the other end?

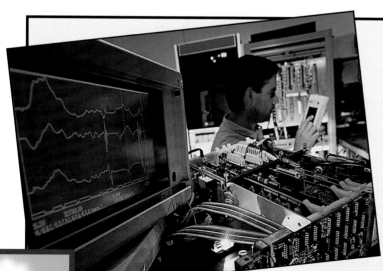

In Action

Vibrations from sound waves that travel through the ground in earthquakes are recorded on special machines called seismographs. Scientists monitor movement of the Earth's plates on these machines so that they can have some idea of when earthquakes are going to occur.

3 Send another wave along the Slinky in the same way as before. Don't lift the Slinky off the table. Look closely to see what happens to the coils as the wave travels along the Slinky.

4 Watch what happens when the wave reaches your friend's end. Does the wave travel in one direction, and then come back? Can you make it come all the way back?

Don't Stop There

● When an object vibrates more quickly, the sound waves traveling from it are more frequent. Watch what happens to the Slinky when you send several waves, one right after another.

Speed of Sound

WHEN YOU HEAR THE BELL ring at the end of recess at school, you hear the sound right away. This is because sound travels quickly from the source of the sound to your ears. Find out more about the speed of sound and how quickly it travels over different distances in this experiment.

✓ **You will need**
- ✓ a toy drum
- ✓ a brightly colored scarf

1 Do this experiment in a quiet, open space. Ask two friends to stand in the middle of your chosen space. Give the drum to one friend (the drummer). Give the scarf to the other (the listener). Ask the listener to walk 20 steps away from the drummer.

2 Stand back so you can see both friends clearly.

In Action

Sound waves travel very fast — about 1,116 ft (340 m) per second in air — but the supersonic transport called the Concorde can travel even faster! At takeoff the Concorde builds up speed, getting faster and faster until it breaks the sound barrier. It is then traveling even faster than the speed of sound! That is why it is called supersonic.

3 Do you think there is a noticeable time gap between a sound being made and a sound being heard? Find out by asking the drummer to bang the drum and the listener to raise the scarf as soon as she or he hears the drum (without looking!). Listen and look closely to see if the drumbeat is heard at the same time it is made. Repeat this step 3 times. What happens?

4 Now ask the listener to walk 20 more steps away from the drummer and repeat the experiment. Does the listener seem to hear the sound as soon as it is made even when the sound is farther away? What does this tell you about the speed of sound?

Don't Stop There

● Now put a ringing alarm clock in the middle of the open space and slowly walk away from it. What happens to the sound? Does it get louder, softer, or stay the same as you get farther away? Walk in a circle around the clock, keeping the same distance away from it this time. Does the sound spread out from the clock in all directions?

How Do We Hear Sounds?

WE HEAR SOUNDS WITH OUR EARS. Our outer ear "collects" the sound waves and funnels them down the ear canal. The sound reaches the eardrum, making it vibrate. This, in turn, causes three tiny ear bones in our middle ear to vibrate. Then little hairs in part of the inner ear called the cochlea vibrate. A special nerve then sends these "vibration messages" to the brain (see diagram on page 17, opposite). Try this experiment to find out more about hearing.

(see diagram on page 17, opposite)

✓ **You will need**
- a tuning fork

1 Ask a friend to sit on a chair in a very quiet place, away from any distracting sounds.

2 Take the tuning fork and bang the forked end on a table edge. The tuning fork will vibrate and make a musical note.

3 Quickly put the end you are holding against your friend's head, just against the entrance to the ear canal. Can your friend hear the note made by the tuning fork? Can he or she hear it well?

4 Repeat this two or three times. How is the sound being heard?

5 Now twang the tuning fork again the same way as before. This time, quickly put the end of the fork on your friend's head, about 2 in. (5 cm) behind the outer ear. Predict what will happen. Can your friend hear the note now? Does it sound the same as it did before? What do you think is happening?

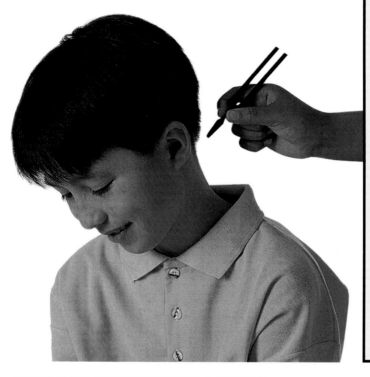

In Action

There are many reasons why some people cannot hear very well. One common reason, especially in children, is a disease called otitis media. Sticky fluid builds up in the middle ear. This stops the eardrum and ear bones from vibrating properly, so sounds cannot be heard well.

Doctors use an instrument called an auriscope (or otoscope) which has a light and a lens, to help them examine people's ears.

Don't Stop There

● Ask your friend to repeat the experiment to see if you can hear the note as well in front of as behind your ear.

● How good is your hearing? Find out by measuring how far away you can hear a pin drop.

Inner ear

Middle ear

Ear bones (ossicles)

Ear canal

Eardrum

Outer ear

Cochlea

Improve Your Hearing!

DO YOU REMEMBER THE STORY "Little Red Riding Hood"? When she saw the wolf in her grandmother's clothes, she exclaimed, "Grandmother, what big ears you have!" The wolf replied, "All the better to hear you with!" Do you think having big ears helps you hear better? Make some big ears and experiment with them to find out.

✓ You will need
- ✓ a large piece of thin cardboard
- ✓ adhesive tape
- ✓ a radio

1 Use the cardboard to make a large cone "ear" to fit over one of your ears.

2 Turn the radio on at a very low volume. Sit a short distance away, and listen carefully.

In Action

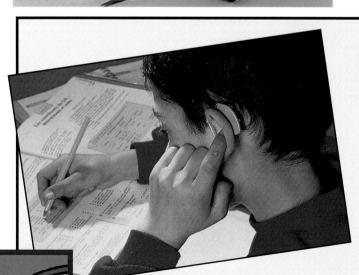

Long ago, animal horns were used to help people hear better, and the first ear trumpets were made in a similar shape. These simple hearing aids used the cone shape to channel the sounds into the ear so that people could hear more clearly. Hearing aids made now use modern technology. They consist of a miniature microphone, amplifier, and loudspeaker.

3 Hold the "big ear" close to one of your ears. Sit in the same place as before and listen to the radio again with your big ear turned toward it. What do you notice about the sound? Does it sound louder, softer, different in any way, or just the same?

4 Try the test a few times to be sure! Did your "big ear" improve your hearing?

Keep Thinking

Have you seen a doctor use a stethoscope? What do you think they are used for?

Don't Stop There

● Do you think the size of the "ear" will make a difference to the loudness of the sound? Try making an even bigger "ear" and a much smaller one. Do the experiment again using each one. What did you find out?

● Do you think the shape of the ear will make a difference to the sound you hear? Try the experiment with ears of different shapes, such as a narrow, pointed one and a short, rounded one. Don't forget to do all the tests the same way to keep it fair. Did the shape of the ear make a difference to the sound you heard?

Loud and Soft

THINK ABOUT HOW YOU MAKE loud sounds or soft sounds. The mine workers in South Africa make loud and soft sounds to accompany a dance using decorated rubber boots. You and your friends can make some decorated boots too, and do your own rubber-boot dance!

✓ You will need

- ✓ a length of elastic (about 3 feet, or 1 meter)
- ✓ a pair of rubber boots to fit you
- ✓ strong thread
- ✓ a selection of items, such as buttons, washers, small bells, paper clips and beads, that can be tied onto the boots to make sounds

1 Cut two lengths of elastic, each one long enough to fit around the leg of the boot with enough extra so that you can tie it on.

2 Tie a piece of elastic fairly tightly around the leg of each boot.

3 Use loops of thread and paper clips to tie the bells, washers, etc., in bundles along the lengths of elastic. Make sure each one can swing freely.

4 Stamp your feet gently and listen to the sound you make. Is it loud or soft? Stamp harder and listen to the sound now. Is it different?

5 Do the rubber-boot dance by dancing and stamping around. Find out what you can do to make loud or soft sounds. Try to make different sounds, for example soft drizzle, rain, and then a storm.

In Action

An oscilloscope shows how a sound wave changes. The picture shows the amplitude (the height) of the sound wave, and how this changes as the sound changes. A tall wave shows a loud sound and a short wave shows a quieter sound. You may have noticed on some machines like CD and cassette players that there is a colored-light display. Lights move up and down as the sound gets louder and softer.

Don't Stop There

● Use junk materials to help you make a very loud clap of thunder. Use the thunder sound and the rubber boots to create the sound effects for a story about a developing storm.

High and Low

In South America, people play a musical instrument called a panpipe. Lots of different notes from high to low can be played on these pipes. Find out about making high and low notes when you make and decorate your very own panpipes.

1 Ask an adult to cut the pipe with the hacksaw into a range of lengths from long to short.

2 Arrange the pieces of pipe next to each other, in order of length. Tape them together and then decorate them.

Keep Thinking

Some animals, such as dogs, can hear higher-pitched sounds than we can. There is a whistle that dogs can hear, but it has too high a pitch for us to hear. Why do you think this might be useful?

Sound waves of high-pitch notes have a higher frequency than low pitched notes. Look back to pages 12 and 13 where you used the Slinky to see how sound waves travel. The quick waves had a higher frequency.

3 First blow over the top of the long pipe. You may need to practice to get a good note.

4 Now blow over the next pipe that is a little bit shorter. What do you notice about the sound? Is the note higher or lower?

5 What kind of note do you think the next pipe will make? Try it and see if you were right. Try blowing over all the other pipes. What do you notice about the notes? Use your panpipe to make up your own tunes.

6 A note that sounds higher or lower than another has a different pitch, or frequency. Why do you think the pitch is different for each pipe?

In Action

Many instruments have tubes of different lengths to change the pitch of the sound. The pitch is changed in a trombone by sliding the tube to make it longer or shorter.

Don't Stop There

● Some instruments have strings that are plucked to make notes. Find some empty cartons in different sizes, some large and some small. Remove the lids and stretch an elastic band over each carton. Twang each band and listen carefully to hear the sound each one makes. What do you notice about the pitch of the notes from each band?

What Does Sound Travel Through?

SOUND TRAVELS THROUGH THE AIR (which is a gas), and this is usually how the sounds we hear come into our ears. But will sound also travel through solid things like string? In this experiment you can make a simple telephone and find out more about what sound travels through.

✓ **You will need**
- ✓ two plastic cups
- ✓ a sharp tool like a skewer or scissors
- ✓ string (about 10 feet, or 3 meters)

1 Ask an adult to help you make a small hole in the base of each cup with the sharp tool.

2 Thread one end of the string through one cup and tie a knot in it, on the inside of the cup. Thread the other end through the other cup and tie it the same way.

3 Ask a friend to hold a cup, walk away from you until the string is tight, and speak quietly into it. While your friend is speaking, hold the other cup next to your ear. Can you hear what is being said through your "telephone"?

In Action

Some sea creatures like dolphins (or whales) send sounds through the water over long distances. They can do this because sound travels so well through water, faster, in fact, than it does through air.

4 Move closer to your friend and try the "telephone" again when the string is not pulled tight. Does your "telephone" work as well?

5 Ask two more friends to join you and make another "telephone." Link the strings together to make a cross in the center and pull the strings tight. Speak into your cup and ask your friends to hold their cups to their ears. Does the sound travel along each of the strings?

Don't Stop There

● Make a simple stethoscope using a length of plastic hose (or tubing) and two funnels. Push one funnel into each end of the hose and use your stethoscope to listen to a friend's heart. Can you hear the heartbeat? What did the sound travel through to get to your ear?

Stop That Noise!

SOMETIMES IT IS NECESSARY to stop sound from traveling — for instance, if the sound is so loud that it could be dangerous, or maybe because the sound is irritating. Would you like peace and quiet to do your homework? Make some earmuffs and find out which material is best to stop that noise!

1 Put the headphones on and turn the stereo on so you can hear the music clearly. (SAFETY! Very loud sounds can damage your ears.)

2 Think about which of your materials will be good at stopping the sound, and arrange them in order of the best to the least soundproof.

Keep Thinking

Think about who might need to protect their ears from loud noises. How do they do it?

3 Choose one material and place a piece of the same thickness next to each ear. Hold it in place with the headphones. Try the other materials in the same way.

4 Keep a record of your results — good to poor soundproofing! Did any material stop the sound completely? Which materials stopped the most sound? Which stopped the least?

5 When sound waves reach a material, some are absorbed and some are reflected away. Only some of the sound gets through. What sort of materials let the most sound through?

Don't Stop There

● Try putting a ticking clock in an empty box. Use different materials to line the box. Put on the lid, and listen each time. Find out which material is best at stopping the sound.

In Action

Loud sounds can be dangerous. Any sound above 140 decibels (the unit of measure for sound) will permanently damage your ears. People who work in very noisy environments, like machine workshops, have to protect their ears. Buildings are often protected from sound with double-glazed windows. The space between the panes of thick glass prevents as much sound as possible from coming through.

Bouncing Sound

Y OU HAVE PROBABLY BOUNCED a ball, but did you know that you can bounce sound too, by reflecting the sound waves? This is known as an echo. Try this experiment and find out more about how sound can be bounced.

1 Start by making two long tubes about 3 inches (8 cm) in diameter, by rolling up each piece of cardboard and securing the loose flap with the tape.

Keep Thinking

Ships at sea use foghorns when it is foggy to find out if there is anything dangerous ahead, such as a cliff or rocks, that they might crash into. How do you think an echo can help them?

2 Lean the metal tray on the table up against a wall and arrange the two long tubes on the table so that they are both at about 45 degrees to the wall.

3 Speak quietly into one tube and ask a friend to listen carefully at the end of the other tube. Can they hear what is being said through the tube? Is the sound clear? How do you think the sound reached your friend's ear? How did the tray help?

In Action

Sound waves we cannot hear, called ultrasound, are used in hospitals to show a picture of a baby inside a mother's womb. The sound wave is sent out and bounced back, and a machine shows the picture on a screen.

Don't Stop There

● The next time you are in a large empty hall or tunnel, shout loudly (if you are allowed to!). What do you hear? What do you think is happening to the sound of your voice?

Glossary

This glossary gives the meaning of each word as it is used in this book.

Absorb A material that absorbs sound soaks it up, and stops some or all of it traveling any further.

Air An invisible mixture of gases, mainly nitrogen and oxygen. Air surrounds the Earth.

Amplifier A machine to make sounds louder.

Amplitude The height of a sound wave. High amplitude sounds are loud, and low amplitude sounds are soft.

Auriscope A medical device used to look inside the ear.

Avalanche A sudden or fast flow of snow or ice down a mountain.

Cochlea The part of the inner ear that converts sound vibrations into messages that are sent by nerves to the brain.

Decibel The loudness of a sound is measured on the Decibel scale.

Ear The organ that enables us to hear sounds and to keep our balance. It consists of three parts — outer, middle, and inner ear.

Ear bones Three tiny bones in the middle ear that vibrate when sound waves hit the eardrum.

Ear canal Part of the outer ear. Sound waves travel down this tube to the middle ear.

Eardrum Separates the outer ear from the middle ear. It is a thin membrane (skin) that vibrates when sound waves hit it.

Earthquake Sudden sharp movements in the Earth's crust, that often cause severe damage.

Echo A sound that is reflected and bounced back to you so you can hear it again.

Frequency The number of waves that travel past a certain point every second. The higher the frequency the higher the pitch.

Gas A gas has no fixed shape or volume. It spreads to fill a container. Often you cannot see gas.

Hearing aid A device used to improve the hearing of partially deaf people by making sounds louder.

Heartbeat The sound your heart makes when it pumps blood around your body.

Liquid A liquid has a definite volume but it can flow and take the shape of the container it is in.

Loud Sounds with high amplitude.

Loud sounds have tall sound waves.
Loudspeaker A machine that converts electrical signals into sound.

Microphone A device that converts sound waves into electrical signals.

Oscilloscope A machine to show the height and frequency of a sound wave.
Otoscope A medical device used to look inside the ear. More usually called an auriscope.

Percussionist A musician who plays instruments, such as drums or cymbals, by hitting or banging them.
Pitch Sound can be high or low pitch. High pitch sound waves travel more frequently than low pitch sound waves.

Reflect When a sound bounces off a surface.

Seismograph A machine that records the sound waves made by movements in the Earth's crust.
Soft Sounds with low amplitude. Soft sounds have short sound waves.
Solid A solid has a definite shape.
Sound source The object or action that is making a sound.
Sound effects Sounds created artificially to mimic real sounds. Used in plays and films.

Sound barrier Resistance in the air that makes it difficult for aircraft to travel faster than sound.
Soundproof To stop sound traveling through an object such as a wall, so that it does not disturb other people.
Speed of sound At an air temperature of 68°C (20°C) sound travels through air at 1,116 feet (340 meters) per second.
Stethoscope A medical device used to listen to your heartbeat.
Supersonic Faster than the speed of sound.

Tuning fork Two-pronged piece of metal that makes a particular musical note when struck.

Ultrasound Very high pitch sound waves that we can't hear. Doctors use ultrasound to look at the inside of the human body, and to take pictures of it. Ultrasound can be used to look at a baby in a womb.

Vibration A fast backward and forward movement.

Womb The place in a woman's body where a baby grows and develops until it is born.

Index